INTRODUCTION

The first homes in Britain were caves or shelters made from brushwood or twigs. People made their own homes for many hundreds of years, using whatever they had: wood, woven sticks, mud cement and thatch for roofs. Some poor people still lived in such simple cottages as late as the 19th century. Wealthy people had bigger and better houses, but few homes – apart from royal palaces – matched the comfort of a Roman villa or the size of a Norman castle. In the 19th century people flocked to work in the new factory towns. Suburbs spread, and in the 20th century new factory-made materials made possible more house-building than ever before.

CONTENTS

CAVES AND CAMPS

The humans who first came to Britain around 40,000 BC were hunters. They lived in caves or camped by rivers in homes made of branches or animal skins. Not until much later did farmers settle and build villages.

Caves like those at Creswell Crags in Derbyshire sheltered people from the bitter cold of the Ice Age in Britain. When the ice melted, around 10,000 years ago, many families stayed in these ready-made homes. Others built new houses from what they could find: mud, wood, stone, turf, sticks and straw.

From about 3500 BC, farmers from Europe came to Britain. Families built homes near each other, for company, to work together and for protection. These homes were the first villages.

▽ **Iron-Age homes** were used for several generations. Some had stone walls. Most had walls of woven branches and mud (known as wattle and daub).

▷ **Some Iron-Age Celtic farmers** built homes with stone walls.
• Such a home had a roof of wooden poles tied together.
• The roof was covered with straw from the fields, tied in bundles.
• The entrance had walls and a door of wood or animal skin.
• A fence around the village protected people and their animals.
• In winter, animals were kept in their owners' homes.
• Old houses were often used as animal shelters.
• Barns and hayricks were built nearby.

To defend their village, people built ditches and banks around it. Inside, as at Windmill Hill in Wiltshire, they lived in homes of wood, with roofs of thatch. Wood rots in the ground, so little is left of these houses today. But some stone houses uncovered by a storm in 1850, at Skara Brae in the Orkney Islands, might have been built between 2000 and 1500 BC. They can still be seen.

By 800 BC, farmers in Britain had started using iron tools. With such tools the people called Celts built fortified settlements, or hillforts, to live in.

△ **Inside Celtic homes** it was dark and there was hardly any furniture. There was a hearth-fire for warmth and cooking. Smoke drifted out through the roof.

▷ **A broch**, or stone house, on the Scottish island of Lewis. Some brochs were 15 metres high. Thick walls protected the people inside from the harsh weather and attack by wild animals and warring neighbours.

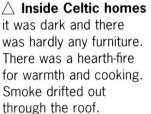

ROMANS AT HOME

The Roman army landed in Britain in AD 43 and housed its soldiers in forts and camps made first of wood, later of stone. As the Romans settled down to govern their new imperial province, they built homes more grand than any before seen in Britain.

Britain grew wealthy under Roman rule and rich Britons also built houses in the Roman style. For the first time, people in Britain could live in towns with piped water, streets of shops and elegant houses, swimming pools, city centres, sports arenas, public parks, temples, statues and fountains.

Roman houses were built of wood, stone and brick. Builders mixed sand, lime and water as mortar to hold bricks together or for plastering walls. For concrete, they added stone chippings to the mixture. Columns were made either from solid stone blocks or from bricks with a coating of plaster.

The wealthiest people in Roman Britain had plumbing in their homes, but most people took water from public troughs in the street. Even rich people had little furniture, apart from beds, couches and folding tables. The floors of fine houses were decorated with mosaics. Their walls were painted with patterns, pictures of birds and flowers, or scenes from myths and legends.

△ **Romans enjoyed bathing.** People went to the mosaic-tiled public bath-houses to relax and meet friends, not just to keep clean.

▽ **Roman builders made walls with bricks** laid around a concrete filling. Or they filled a wooden framework with stones or mortar, then plastered the surface.

◁ **Roman soldiers lived in barracks**, like these at a milecastle on Hadrian's Wall. Up to a hundred troops lived in the buildings, which were made using local stone.

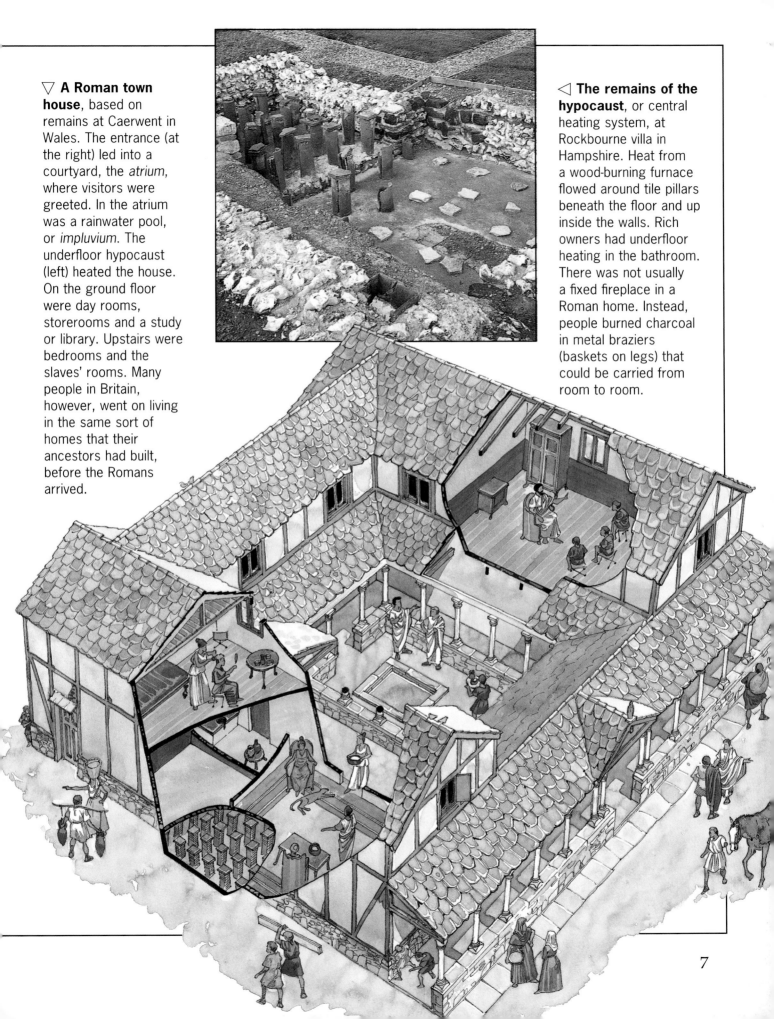

▽ **A Roman town house**, based on remains at Caerwent in Wales. The entrance (at the right) led into a courtyard, the *atrium*, where visitors were greeted. In the atrium was a rainwater pool, or *impluvium*. The underfloor hypocaust (left) heated the house. On the ground floor were day rooms, storerooms and a study or library. Upstairs were bedrooms and the slaves' rooms. Many people in Britain, however, went on living in the same sort of homes that their ancestors had built, before the Romans arrived.

◁ **The remains of the hypocaust**, or central heating system, at Rockbourne villa in Hampshire. Heat from a wood-burning furnace flowed around tile pillars beneath the floor and up inside the walls. Rich owners had underfloor heating in the bathroom. There was not usually a fixed fireplace in a Roman home. Instead, people burned charcoal in metal braziers (baskets on legs) that could be carried from room to room.

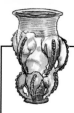

SAXON HOUSES AND HALLS

As the Romans left Britain, starting around AD 400, so new farming peoples from Europe moved in and built settlements of sturdy timber houses. Their leaders carved out kingdoms for themselves, rewarding their followers at feasts in royal halls.

The newcomers – Saxons, Angles, Franks, Frisians and Jutes among them – settled in clusters of farms. They felled trees to clear farmland and used the wood to build homes. Their houses were oblong, with just one room shared by the family and a few animals in winter.

▽ **In a Saxon village**, houses and animal pens were clustered inside a wooden fence. Log pathways were laid across muddy ground.

▷ **The great hall of a Saxon noble or king** had a high, sloped roof supported by long wooden beams. A great hall might have a roof of tiles or wooden shingles, but ordinary people's homes were usually thatched with straw.

◁ **A reconstruction of an Anglo-Saxon hall** at West Stow in Suffolk.

▽ **Inside a Saxon house**, women cooked meat or fish in an iron pot hung over the fire, and baked their own bread. People made their own pottery and wove their own cloth. Iron knives, bone combs and decorated drinking cups and jars, like those shown left, might be bought from a trader at the local market.

A fire burned in the centre of the room, but there was no chimney and so the rooms must have been very smoky. Floors were of beaten earth, perhaps strewn with rushes, or were dug out and covered by wooden boards. The roof was thatched with dried straw, reeds, heather or wattle, and it sloped steeply.

The biggest houses were the Saxon leaders' halls, which were the centre of the community. Even these great houses had just one room, divided by wicker partitions into sections for living, sleeping and for livestock. At night, the king went to his chamber while his followers slept in the hall where they had just feasted. "A great band of earls occupied the hall... they cleared away the bench-boards; it was spread over with beds and bolsters [pillows]", says the author of *Beowulf*.

There was little furniture apart from benches and trestle tables. A large hall might be decorated with carvings or textile wall hangings; ordinary families used animal skins to keep warm.

VIKING AGE HOMES

In AD 866, Vikings from Scandinavia took York (Eoforwic) from the Northumbrians. Many settlers soon swelled the town they called Jorvik ('Wild Boar Creek'). New streets were built and regular building plots laid out. Jorvik and Dublin in Ireland were bustling centres of trade.

▽ **Viking houses lined the streets of Jorvik.** Each house probably had a shop or stall at the front selling goods made in a workshop built behind the house.

◁ **Important churches and monasteries,** like Jarrow in Northumbria, were made of stone. The Christian monks lived and worked together, growing food, copying books, teaching and praying in the church. Saxon churches had rounded arches above windows and doorways.

▷ **Streets in Viking towns were noisy, smelly and smoky.** At the back of houses were storage pits, rubbish pits, wells and cesspits for toilet waste. Geese, hens and a pig or two might be kept in the back yard.

Houses on the streets of York stood on plots of land divided by wattle fences. Viking houses were small and made of wood, like those of the Anglo-Saxons. Before about 950, many York homes had walls of wattle, woven around upright posts and weather-proofed by daub plaster. Each building was at least 6.8 metres long and 4.4 metres wide. The wattle was usually of willow or hazel and the roof probably of thatch, laid on a frame of poles and branches.

▷ **Viking town houses had wooden frames and straw or turf roofs.** Towns were often built near water so that trade goods could be unloaded from ships. The remains of the wooden posts of some Viking houses at Jorvik have been preserved in water-logged ground.

There was only one room and little furniture. Along the walls were earth-filled wattle benches. Blankets and furs to keep people warm at night were stowed by day in a big wooden chest. In the centre of the earth floor stood a hearth for the fire, marked out with stones, logs or even old Roman tiles.

Around 970, new houses were built with dug-out floors. Strong oak planks lined the sides of the 'cellar' and some homes had floorboards laid on joists (supports). Viking builders also found ways of keeping homes warm by using double walls or lining them with woven twigs to reduce heat loss.

△ **Remains of a 9th-century Viking farmer's hall-house** at Jarlshof in the Shetlands.

▽ **Outdoor toilets** had wattle walls and a board with a hole for a seat.

NEW BUILDERS, NEW METHODS

In 1066 England was conquered by the Normans, who were great builders in stone. "In times past, men were contented to dwell in houses builded of... willow, plumtree... elme, so that the use of y oake was in maner dedicated wholie unto churches."

▷ (Below) **The first Norman castles** were wooden towers built on earth mounds or mottes.
• A castle like this could be built in two weeks.
• The tower was covered with ox-hides. When soaked with water they protected the tower from fire when attacked.
• Within the castle enclosure, or bailey, there were houses for soldiers and their families.
• There were also store-houses, a kitchen and stables for the horses.
• Outside the fence other houses were built, the beginnings of a new village.

▷ **A cathedral, a house of God.** While the houses of the poor changed little under the Normans, only the finest building materials were used for churches and cathedrals. Religious buildings and castles became lasting memorials to the medieval builders.

The Normans brought new building methods to Britain. They built castles to guard their lands, and great cathedrals. The early castles were grim, cold and uncomfortable homes. There was little furniture, apart from benches and tables, stools and a chest for storing valuables. The lord had a bed with a feather mattress, bolster (pillow), linen sheets and a fur coverlet. But his followers slept on the floor. There was a fire, but draughts blew in through windows, which might have shutters but no glass.

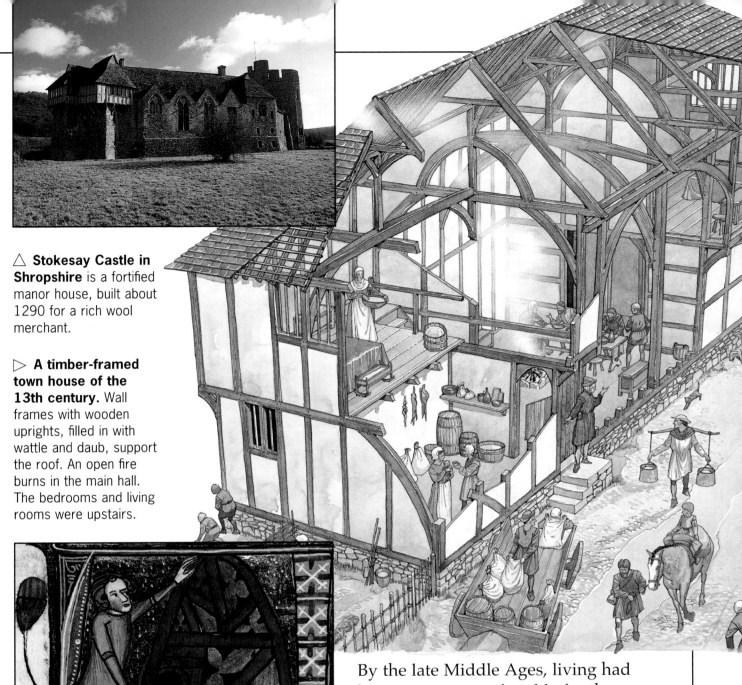

△ **Stokesay Castle in Shropshire** is a fortified manor house, built about 1290 for a rich wool merchant.

▷ **A timber-framed town house of the 13th century.** Wall frames with wooden uprights, filled in with wattle and daub, support the roof. An open fire burns in the main hall. The bedrooms and living rooms were upstairs.

◁ **New engineering techniques**, such as flying buttresses, were used to support high stone buildings. Masons, carpenters and glaziers worked from scaffolding.

△ **Wood was the basic material** for a medieval 'cruck' house. Trees were split to make curved (crooked) arches, a pair of which held up the roof beam.

By the late Middle Ages, living had become more comfortable for the landowner. His manor house had more than one bedroom, and tapestries hung on its stone walls. The kitchen was joined to the house by a hallway, so food was still warm by the time servants brought it to their master's table.

Medieval towns grew bigger. Within the town walls, houses of all different shapes and sizes were squashed together. Rooms were built on as needed, making the streets crowded and unhealthy.

HOME COMFORTS

By William Shakespeare's time, in the late 16th century, many people in the countryside and towns were growing more prosperous. They spent money on bigger and better homes – houses with chimneys and staircases, and more home comforts indoors.

Thousands of new homes were built in the 16th and early 17th centuries. They were warmer, with wood panelling on the walls. They had more furniture and an inside staircase. They were bigger, with more rooms. A peasant's cottage might now have a separate bedroom, or bower, even though the living room was still likely to have a stable at one end.

New homes had a brick fireplace set into the wall, with a hood to lead away the smoke up a brick chimney. Farmhouses and townhouses often had two storeys, with a wooden staircase to the upper rooms. Many townhouses included a workshop where the owner carried on his trade.

△ **Tudor town houses** were often close to medieval walls. Even in Tudor times, old town walls were still repaired as a defence against possible attack by foreign armies.

◁ **Tudor tiled-roofed and timber-framed houses** at Lavenham, in Suffolk. Inside a Tudor home, the wood panels and the oak furniture made rooms dark. On the floor, people spread rushes, lavender or rush mats. Carpets, rare before 1570, were hung on the walls for show.

◁ **Many people lived in villages.** The houses overlooked the green, where children played and people met to exchange news and gossip. In most villages, the windmill (for grinding corn into flour) and the church were the biggest of all the buildings.

The 'Tudor' style of building is familiar to us, because it was often copied by later builders. It used a mixture of timber and brick. Most houses had a framework of wood, usually oak, but bricks were now often cheaper to use instead. Local stone was also used when available, for example in Scotland.

Many houses were 'half-timbered', with plasterwork panels filling the wooden frame. There were more rooms, each with its own use: a parlour for entertaining, a dining room, bedrooms and kitchen.

▷ **Houses on London Bridge** in Shakespeare's London. There were shops, too, crammed on to the bridge, and even a prison. Privies (toilets) in the houses were built out above the water.

▷ **Building a house**
required the skills of a carpenter, bricklayer, stonemason and plasterer.

• Wooden scaffolding was put up during building work.

• Most houses before about 1570 had only three rooms. After that, four or five rooms became usual.

• One of the rooms was the kitchen, and there were brick fireplaces.

• The lavatory was still an outside privy.

• Inside, the master and mistress sat on chairs. Children and servants had stools or benches.

• Manor houses had separate parlours, dining rooms and bedrooms.

• A long corridor took the place of the old great hall.

• Windows were made of glass panels, held in place by strips of lead.

15

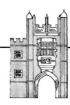

MANORS AND MANSIONS

Henry VIII set a new trend by building grand palaces. He sold off monastery lands to wealthy families, who built fine houses on their new estates. Country gentlemen and rich merchants demanded homes on which no expense was spared.

Among the great houses of the time were Hampton Court (1514-36), Hardwick Hall (1597), built for Bess of Hardwick, and Hatfield House, rebuilt between 1607 and 1611 for the Earl of Salisbury. These homes were far grander than any in Britain since Roman times, with their impressive pointed gables, bay windows and tall chimneys. Many large houses were built in the half-timbered style, but by the early 17th century, stone was increasingly thought more fitting for a country mansion.

▷ **Large country houses** had neatly laid out gardens, with hedges and paths, in which people could stroll and children play.

▽ **Hampton Court** was a splendid house beside the River Thames. One of the finest of King Henry VIII's palaces, its extravagant style symbolized the new age.

△ **Inside Melford Hall in Suffolk.** This Tudor mansion, built in brick, has changed little since 1578. This view of the original banqueting hall shows Tudor panelled walls, furniture, fireplace and paintings.

The great houses had imposing entrances, with 'wings' or blocks on either side. The hall was no longer the centre of family life. Now the finest room was upstairs – a long gallery which ran the whole length of the house. Here family and guests could walk on rainy days, or sing and play music.

Houses were no longer built like fortresses. There were more home comforts: oak chairs and tables, paintings and tapestries on the walls, and four-poster beds with curtains to pull round at night. There was fine wood carving on staircases, doors and panels. The ceilings, too, were decorated with plaster patterns.

◁ **A great Tudor house**, like Little Moreton Hall in Cheshire, had dark but splendid rooms inside. Often wood panels were painted with scenes, or the walls were hung with tapestry. Window glass was still rare and found only in such grand houses. Wealthy people took their glass with them when they moved house.

◁ **Hengrave Hall in Suffolk** is visited by Queen Elizabeth I, who arrives in a litter. Such royal visits strained the resources of even the wealthiest landowner. Elizabeth travelled with as many as 1,000 courtiers and servants, all of whom had to be given food and shelter.

STONE AND BRICK

Many of London's old wooden houses burned down in the Great Fire of 1666. People had been used to building houses as they pleased. Now new buildings were often planned by architects in the 'Classical' style. They built in stone and brick, not wood.

△ **The new buildings** were made of brick and stone, with tiled roofs.

△ **A stone and brick house** in Cranborne, Dorset. The manor house was a gift to the powerful Cecil family from King James I.

Before the Great Fire, London was like many cities in Europe – crowded and rat-infested. The rebuilt city had Sir Christopher Wren's great churches and also the brick town houses he designed.

Some of the most splendid homes in Britain were built by the new architects, such as Blenheim Palace in Oxfordshire and Chatsworth House in Derbyshire. Inside, Grinling Gibbons carved flowers and fruit in wood. Outside, Capability Brown laid out parks and gardens.

The rich houses of the new age were plainer in shape than Tudor palaces, but not plainly decorated. In smaller houses, the front door opened into an entrance hall leading to the staircase. Rooms were cosier, with padded armchairs instead of wooden stools and benches.

◁ **The Great Fire** destroyed more than 13,000 homes in London. The city's old wooden houses were built close together in narrow streets, and flames leapt from one thatched roof to the next. From the ashes of old London, bold plans for a new city emerged but were only partly carried out.

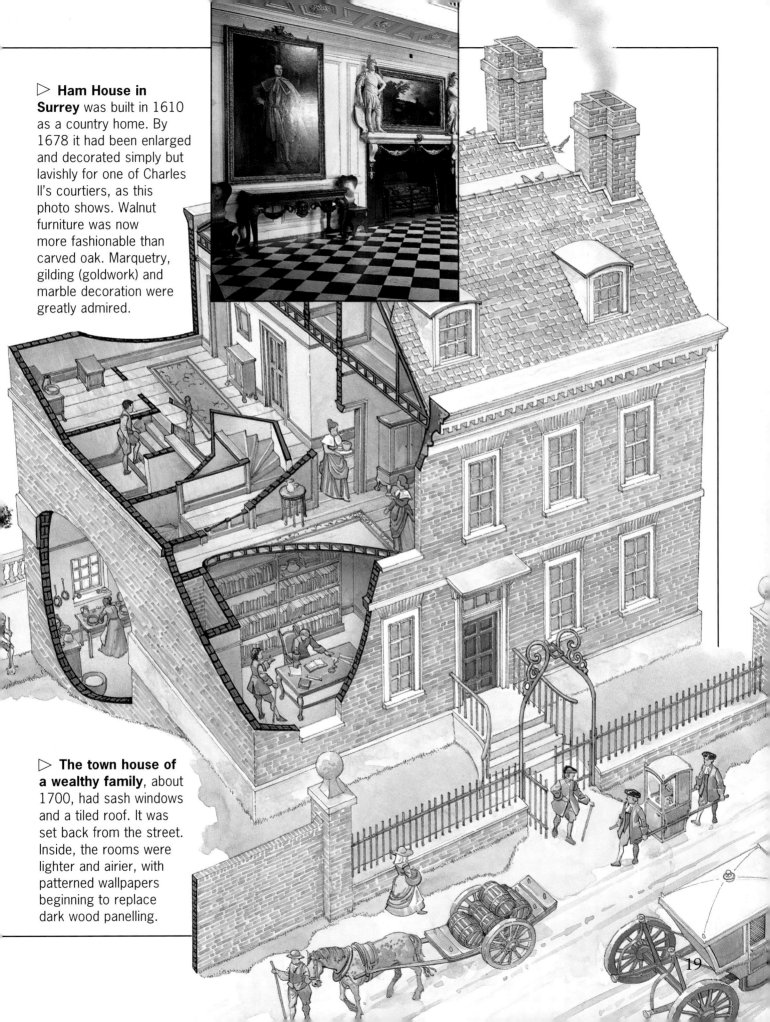

▷ **Ham House in Surrey** was built in 1610 as a country home. By 1678 it had been enlarged and decorated simply but lavishly for one of Charles II's courtiers, as this photo shows. Walnut furniture was now more fashionable than carved oak. Marquetry, gilding (goldwork) and marble decoration were greatly admired.

▷ **The town house of a wealthy family**, about 1700, had sash windows and a tiled roof. It was set back from the street. Inside, the rooms were lighter and airier, with patterned wallpapers beginning to replace dark wood panelling.

TOWN AND COUNTRY

By the 18th century, grand country houses were being built. In the towns, houses were being arranged in squares, terraces and crescents. But many poor homes still had "a hovel-like appearance far from agreeable", according to a visitor to Lancashire in 1815.

The stylish squares and terraces of Georgian towns like Bath were now laid out to a plan. Most houses were tall and narrow, but two rooms deep, with steps up from the pavement to the door. The kitchen and scullery were in the basement. Servants slept in the attic.

Stone was often used as a main building material, or for facing and decoration. Tall windows let light into rooms in which there were colourful wallpapers, marble fireplaces with coal fires, mirrors, rugs and panelled doors.

Many country houses reflected the growing prosperity of their owners. But most farmworkers still lived in tiny cottages. As the Industrial Revolution began, the first of thousands of cheap, poorly-made workers' homes were built around new ironworks and coal mines.

▽ **A stately home** was the centre of an estate which the owner could rule like a medieval baron. Gamekeepers set traps for poachers stealing his animals.

△ **Poor homeless people** had to beg on the streets or live in a workhouse. Each district had its own workhouse, where men and women lived separately.

◁ **Inside the huge kitchen of St. James's Palace in London** at the time of King George III. Large windows let in plenty of light.

◁ **Many Georgian town houses were built of red brick.** In the tiled roof, a small window lets light into the servants' rooms. There are a lot of stairs for the servants to climb! The grand reception and dining rooms have elegant chairs and tables, made by such fashionable 'cabinet-makers' as Chippendale, Hepplewhite and Sheraton. Many older houses were given new fronts in the Georgian style to make them look up-to-date.

▽ **The Circus in Bath**, a long sweep of houses for doctors, lawyers and merchants, was designed by John Wood. He wanted whole groups of buildings to look attractive. Rebuilding made 18th-century Bath a very fashionable town.

21

WEALTHY VICTORIANS

Many Victorians who grew rich in industrial Britain built big new houses. They copied earlier styles, such as Tudor and Gothic (medieval), and filled their rooms with rich furnishings. A houseful of servants was needed to run such homes.

▽ **An end-of-terrace suburban house**, about 1880. Moulded brick windows and balconies were popular features. Heat came from coal fires, cleared and relit daily by servants. Coal was stored in a cellar beneath the house.

▷ **Front gardens** were new in towns, though many country cottages had them.

△ **Victorian rooms can look overcrowded to us.** People liked to display their favourite mementoes and ornaments. Potted plants were fashionable, and family photographs were to be found in many homes.

▽ **Victorians liked novelties.** People soon began installing the new telephone (invented in 1876). Flush toilets were fitted in many new homes as standards of hygiene rose.

Victorians did not build in one style. They liked romantic and picturesque homes, with patterned brick walls, turrets, battlements and pointed arches and windows. Very rich people built imposing brick mansions in the country and in towns.

Houses for the better off were also built on the outskirts of towns, creating new suburbs. Some stood alone as detached homes, while others formed part of a row. With their balconies and iron railings, these solid-looking homes might now have bathrooms, lavatories and hot water. Most people, however, still made do with a washstand in the bedroom. Gas-lighting became common, replacing candles or oil lamps.

In the kitchen, a range that heated both oven and hot water replaced the open fire. Parlours and drawing rooms were filled with chairs, sofas and tables covered with heavy cloths. Windows were ornately draped with sets of thick and lace curtains. Wallpapers were heavily patterned and all around was a clutter of family photographs, pot plants, china ornaments, even glass cases of waxed fruit or stuffed animals.

△ **Osborne House on the Isle of Wight** was a favourite royal home. Here, Queen Victoria preferred middle-class comfort to palatial luxury.

▽ **A family Christmas.** Traditions such as the fir tree, decorations and Christmas cards were introduced or revived by the Victorians.

WORKING-CLASS HOMES

Victorian workers' homes were mostly small and overcrowded. "Families live in cellars and kitchens of these undrained houses, dark and extremely damp," commented the Poor Law Commissioners visiting a London street in 1838.

◁ **In this worker's home**, about 1880, the living room is also the kitchen where there is a coal-burning range. Washing is done in the scullery. There is no bathroom and the toilet is outside, next to the coal shed. The house is lit by gaslight. With only a tiny yard for children to play in, people had little privacy.

△ **These Victorian workers' homes** in Birmingham still housed families in 1955. The houses had changed little since Victorian times. They were knocked down in the 1960s.

△ **Estates of 'model dwellings'** like these in London were paid for by wealthy men like American banker George Peabody. They provided decent and affordable homes for working people.

The rapid growth of factories meant that new houses had to be built in industrial towns for factory workers to rent. Rows of small brick houses spread out across the countryside, as many homes as possible were crowded together. Terraced houses were squashed back to back, with no garden but just a yard with wash-houses and toilets shared by several families. Most houses had four small rooms, 'two up, two down'. Tall narrow tenement blocks were packed with city families like crowded birds' nests. People called them 'rookeries'.

Badly-built houses with leaking roofs and rotten timbers soon became slums, their broken windows patched with paper or old sacks. Many farmworkers lived in 'tied' cottages owned by the farmer: for them, losing their job meant losing their home.

Homeless people, including children on their own, slept rough on the streets. The dreadful conditions bred disease, crime and misery. The government and local councils began improvements by putting in drains and clean water supplies, and building schools and parks. However, as the 19th century ended, millions of people still lived in slums.

△**Cramped workers' houses were built beside factories** in the industrial regions, shown on the map above.
• Workers' houses were built in dreary rows with narrow alleys between.
• Houses were crowded.
• Many families were large: six children was the Victorian average.
• People walked to work as there was no public transport.
• Men came round early in the morning to 'knock up' people for work by tapping on windows.
• Even at home, people could not get away from the smells, noise and dirt of the factories.

25

SEMI-DETACHED HOMES

In the first half of the 20th century, the demand for homes rose constantly. Governments built millions of houses and created new towns. More people now owned their homes and bought factory-made furniture and new labour-saving appliances.

After the First World War (1914-18), the British government began to replace city slums with new council houses, usually arranged in large estates. The first tall blocks of council flats rose skywards.

Even more houses were needed after the Second World War (1939-45). New towns were built, with shops, schools, parks and other amenities. Many of the people who came to these new towns had lived in inner-city slums.

By the 1950s more and more people lived in the suburbs, travelling into town centres to work. Many new private houses were 'semi-detached' (two houses joined together), which were cheaper than single (detached) houses.

▽ **Without servants**, better-off people bought equipment like the cooker in this poster of 1929. After an evening out, a couple finds supper ready in the oven.

▷ **Home life in the 1940s** for many people was a struggle against shortages. This 1946 family sit close to the fire on wooden chairs. There is no television, though most people listened to the 'wireless' (radio). There is a rag rug on the floor and a curtain over the door to keep out cold draughts. In the years after the Second World War, shops had little to sell, and many goods were still rationed.

▷ **A suburban 'semi' in the 1930s** was built of brick with a tiled roof and wooden window frames. The diamond-shaped panes in bay (box-shaped) windows were a common feature. Electricity and gas were supplied, but most rooms were still heated by coal fires.

◁ **Suburban living** offered greater home comforts for ordinary people than ever before. People in new homes enjoyed running water in their bathroom and kitchen, and an indoor lavatory. They had gardens where children could play. More people could afford vacuum cleaners, telephones and other gadgets. More families owned cars, too.

△ **The massive house-building of the 1920s and 1930s** created a new suburban landscape around many cities. Good transport links meant that people could travel further to work. The new suburban houses were the most sought-after in Britain. Building societies and banks lent money to help people buy houses and share in the comfortable new life that 'suburbia' seemed to offer.

▷ **Saving precious belongings** from a bombed house during the Second World War. Bombing left many families homeless.

MODERN HOUSING

Many more people in Britain want flats or houses of their own than ever before. Old towns grow bigger. New towns are created. Housing people in decent, affordable homes in a pleasant, safe environment is one of today's big issues.

▽ **Moving to homes in new towns**, like Hemel Hempstead, gave many people from the inner cities their first chance to discover the pleasure of gardening.

Much of the rebuilding of the 1950s and 1960s was ill thought-out and hasty. Some people housed 'temporarily' in prefabricated dwellings were still living in them 20 years later.

Mistakes were made in planning some new towns and housing estates. Open spaces, shops and recreation facilities were often inadequate. In particular, there were problems with some multi-storey tower blocks that proved unsuitable for families with children. Some of these early high-rise buildings were so badly built that they were later found to be unsafe and had to be pulled down. Few such blocks are built today.

▽ **In the 1960s, high-rise blocks were built in cities** to rehouse people whose old terraced homes were demolished. Factory-made sections were fixed together on site, reducing construction time and costs.

▷ **Modern houses at Burgess Hill, Sussex.** More houses are needed every year, including family homes like these, city-centre apartments, and retirement homes. New communities need schools, hospitals and utilities (water, power, rubbish collection and so on). They also need transport links. Usually this means roads, but cycle tracks, railways and tramways offer alternatives to prevent worsening traffic jams.

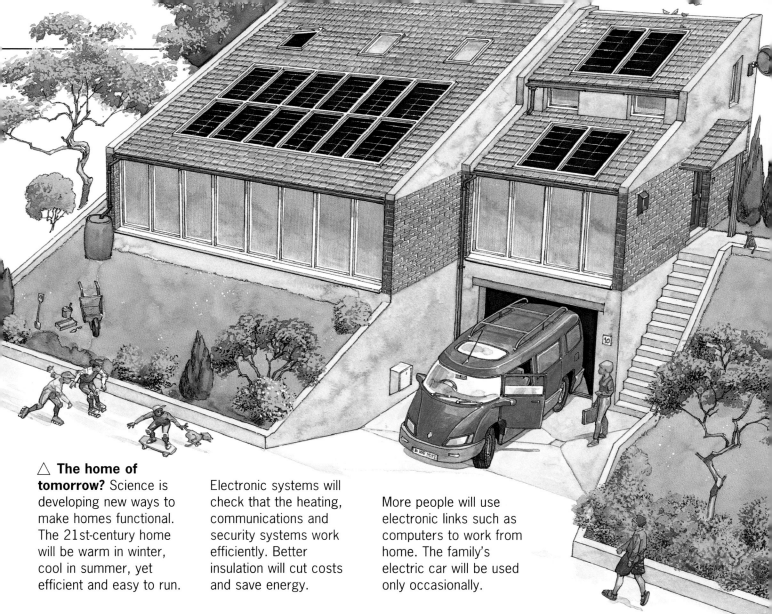

△ **The home of tomorrow?** Science is developing new ways to make homes functional. The 21st-century home will be warm in winter, cool in summer, yet efficient and easy to run.

Electronic systems will check that the heating, communications and security systems work efficiently. Better insulation will cut costs and save energy.

More people will use electronic links such as computers to work from home. The family's electric car will be used only occasionally.

Most new or renovated homes are provided by private builders or housing associations, for people who wish to buy their own house or flat. Others are made available for rent.

Today, a new home is built to be energy-efficient. Its windows are double-glazed and it is well insulated. Heating is usually by gas or electricity, although solar cells and other alternative energy sources are also being used.

Modern homes contain dishwashers, computers, stereos, microwaves, TVs and other equipment that would have amazed house-owners of the 1950s.

PLACES TO VISIT

You can find examples of houses and homes from different periods of history all over the British Isles. Here are just a few suggestions for museums and houses to visit. Your local tourist office will be able to tell you about other places in your area.

The Argory, County Tyrone, Northern Ireland. Victorian house and furniture.

Blenheim Palace, Woodstock, Oxfordshire. Georgian home of the Duke of Marlborough built in the early 1700s.

Buckingham Palace, London. Modernized by Queen Victoria.

Burghley House, Cambridgeshire. Tudor home of the Cecil family.

Chatsworth House, Derbyshire. Stuart architecture and furnishings and Inigo Jones designs.

Chedworth, Gloucestershire. Remains of a Roman villa.

Hampton Court, near London. Tudor palace with famous gardens and maze.

Hardwick Hall, Derbyshire. Good example of a grand Elizabethan house.

Highland Folk Museum, Kingussie, Scotland. Copies of 18th-century houses.

Ightham Mote, Kent. Moated manor house from 1340.

Imperial War Museum, London. Exhibits include features on the bombing during the Second World War.

Jorvik Viking Centre, York. Recreates life in a Viking town, with reconstructions of houses.

Little Moreton Hall, Cheshire. Example of half-timbered buildings.

North of England Open Air Museum, Beamish, County Durham. Reconstructions of houses, including a miner's cottage.

Royal Crescent, Bath, Avon. Curved row of Georgian houses designed by John Wood and built in 1767-74.

Skara Brae, Orkney. Stone Age village which shows how people lived and ate.

Stowe Landscape Gardens, Buckinghamshire. Georgian gardens.

Ulster History Park, Co. Tyrone. Reconstructions of Ulster life from 8000 BC.

Victoria and Albert Museum, London. Good displays of costume and furniture.

Weald and Downland Museum, Sussex. Examples of medieval houses, farms and rural buildings.

Welsh Folk Museum, Cardiff. Reconstructions of farmworker's cottage and other old buildings.

West Stow, Suffolk. Reconstruction of a Saxon village.

FURTHER READING

A Victorian Street, Richard Wood, Wayland, 1993.
A Victorian Village, Martin Parsons, Wayland, 1995.
Castles and Mansions, Alan James, Wayland, 1988.
Daily Life in a Tudor House, Laura Wilson, Heinemann 1995.
Daily Life in a Victorian House, Laura Wilson, Heinemann 1995.
Daily Life in a Wartime House, Laura Wilson, Heinemann 1995.
Exploring Houses and Homes, Cliff Lines, Wayland, 1989.
History from Objects in the Home, Karen Bryant-Mole, Wayland, 1993.
History of Britain: Life in a Viking Town, Brenda Williams, Heinemann, 1997.
History of Britain: Roman Villas, Brenda Williams, Heinemann, 1997.
Homes, John Foster, Hodder and Stoughton, 1990.
Rooms Through the Ages, (series), Watts.
Tudor Palaces and Other Great Houses, Andrew Langley, Heinemann, 1997.

GLOSSARY

cabinet-maker A person skilled in making furniture.

citizens People of a town or city.

council A group of people who run a district.

council house A home built by a local council for people to rent.

estate An area on which many houses or flats are built; originally a large area of land, with farms, owned by one person.

factory A place where people use machines to help them manufacture, or make, a product.

gable A triangular shape between the wall and sloping roof of a house.

household All the people living in a house, including servants.

master In the 19th century and earlier, the man who owned a house and was head of a family or business.

merchants People who make their living by buying and selling things.

monarch A king or queen.

mortgage A loan from a bank or building society to help a person buy a property.

mosaic A design on a floor or wall made from small pieces of stone or glass.

noble A local ruler or landowner, known by a title (such as 'lord').

range A combined fire and oven, heated by burning wood or coal.

scullery A room in a 19th-century house, with a sink for washing.

sewer A drain for dirty water.

slum A part of a town with poorly built and overcrowded houses.

suburb A built-up area on the edge of a town.

tapestry A woven wall covering, for decoration.

tenement A tall building containing homes for many families.

villa In Roman times, a farm with house and outbuildings, or a country house; in Victorian times, a popular term for a middle-class home.

workhouse A building in which poor people were fed and housed in return for doing some work.

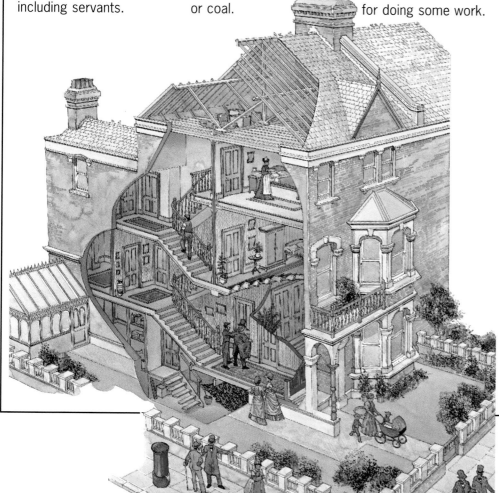

Index